Great Shakes

Great Shakes

Salts and Peppers for All Tastes

BY GIDEON BOSKER

Photographs by Gideon Bosker and Miriam Seger

Abbeville Press • Publishers • New York

Editor: Sarah Kirshner
Design: Howard Morris
Production: Hope Koturo

Library of Congress Cataloging-in-Publication Data

Bosker, Gideon.
    Great shakes.

    1. Salt and pepper shakers.   2. Salt and pepper
shakers—Collectors and collecting—United States.
3. Novelties.   I. Title.
NK8640.B67   1986   730   85-26764
ISBN 0-89659-608-7

First edition, second printing

Contents

Introduction

My romance with salt and pepper shakers began with a harmless voyeuristic act on a hot tin roof. One blistering summer afternoon, my friend Lena and I were shooting photographs of a nineteenth-century cast-iron building for a book on Portland architecture. After finishing the shot, we took a last long look around to be sure that we hadn't missed any other architectural musts. As we scanned the urban landscape, our eyes stopped at a third-floor window across the street. Through the parted curtains, we caught a glimpse of a wall of shelves packed with several hundred salt and pepper shakers. From a distance, the collection looked like a giant multi-colored crystal. It was love at first sight. We made note of the apartment's location, dismantled our camera and headed for the lobby. We rang the appropriate buzzer and within moments, Mattie, a sweet elderly woman, appeared at the door. "We noticed your salt and pepper collection from the rooftop," we offered by way of introduction. "C'mon in," she said. And the rest is history.

Mattie's apartment was one vast salt and pepper installation. Displayed in thematic groupings that ran the gamut from prehistoric animals to space ships, Mattie's collection occupied nearly one-half of her tiny flat. "This was my first set," she explained pointing to a pair of plastic root beer floats. "My son gave them to me as a birthday present in 1949, and I've been collecting shakers ever since." Scanning the sets in Mattie's collection filled us with the kind of delight one usually experiences in a museum or candy store. Fashioned from chalk, metal, glass, plastic, and porcelain, her collection covered all the bases of contemporary culture from space needles and cartoon characters to Greyhound buses and rock 'n' roll. "Now let me see," she continued while pointing out individual sets. "I got these ceramic flamingoes in the Everglades in 1968, and I picked up this metal set of Niagara Falls in 1952. . . . It's very rare. My friend sent me this Canadian Mountie and horse from British Columbia." She knew the vital statistics for every set in her collection. We asked Mattie which pair she used on her kitchen table. "The one over there," she said, pointing to a carton of Morton salt.

We left Mattie's apartment feeling that we had been introduced to a rich, yet virtually unexplored, vein in the history of American vernacular art. We also left with a new obsession—collecting salt and pepper shakers. In fact, on our next car trip across the Pacific Northwest, Lena and I pursued salt and pepper sets with the assiduousness of bounty hunters. At thrift stores, flea markets, and upscale antique stores, we purchased just about every shaker that caught our eye. Finding shakers of such architectural monuments as the Empire State Building, the Space Needle, and Trylon and Perisphere became an obsession. We began trading our booty with other collectors the way kids trade baseball cards. After exhausting the architectural theme, our interest turned to plastic shakers from the 1940s and quirky souvenir shakers in all shapes and forms. Before long, every window sill, bookshelf, and cabinet in sight was overflowing with salt and peppers. Our house had turned into a Noah's Ark of pop culture. Most collectors will recount similar stories of delirious expansion.

Within a year of our visit to Mattie, we had met collectors with as many as 5,400 shakers and found ourselves at the hub of a salt and pepper network that extended from coast to coast. After visiting and documenting more than fifty collections, we thought we'd seen it all. But we were wrong. We learned there is no such thing as a jaded salt and pepper collector. This is a decorative world that's always filled with surprises. No matter how many shakers we've seen over the years, a set or two always crops up that we've never seen before. Ten thousand shakers later, this is still true.

But that's only part of the magic of salt and peppers. The other part is their universal appeal, and, of course, the people who collect them. They are a zany and eccentric bunch. We met Larry, executive editor of a New York publishing house, who had filled the walls of his summer house with more than 600 pairs. Alligators were his specialty. There was Delrae, a third-generation collector, who had amassed a 2,400-piece collection rich in birds and prehistoric animals. Dawn, an antique dealer, collected farm animals and Disney characters. Barbara, a graphic artist, specialized in plasticware, fruitheads, and domestic appliances. And Marcia, the director of a New York museum, had been collecting shakers for more than fifteen years. We found that most collectors confessed to having a passion for a particular shaker type or theme group. Rich or poor, high brow or philistine, it became clear that few could resist the magic of the humble object that has tickled the imagination of so many anonymous designers in such varied ways.

As we made the rounds of collections across the country, we tried to pin down the source of their elusive appeal. The eclectic beauty of shakers is certainly part of every collector's story. But to our way of thinking, the capacity shakers have for shrinking the complex web of human endeavors and obsessions into a miniature and, fortunately, very affordable world is just as intriguing. What's more, we'd never seen utilitarian novelties in which form so completely and exuberantly ignores function.

But we learned that this is only part of their irresistible charm. Quirky, kinky, or parodic, shakers are guaranteed to fascinate both the neophyte and well-seasoned connoisseur. And except for the basic requirements of a small chamber, entrance hole, and exit port, salt and pepper shakers can mimic virtually any object, man-made, natural, or fanciful. That's what makes them ideal exhibits for privately curated museums. For most collectors, shakers are an intimate link to an America on the move. Almost without exception, we found that salt and peppers rekindled in their owners the magic of a skyscraper or monument they once visited, a vacationland paradise that exhilarated them, or the sensibilities of an aesthetic movement that captured their imaginations. In a sense, then, shakers brought their owners a double dose of the spice of life. Collectors ingested their bounty not only to flavor food but to replenish themselves with visual memories of landmarks no longer within reach. For us, as well as for aficionados, shakers became street signs for memory lane.

Contemporary shakers have come a long way since the generic saltcellar, a small and undistinguished vessel or dish used since ancient times for storing salt. Of course, some saltcellars were ornamental masterpieces that graced the tables of the wealthy. Perhaps the most celebrated such saltcellar was made in 1543 for King Francis I by the Florentine goldsmith and sculptor Benvenuto Cellini. In many respects, this elaborate gold saltcellar can be seen as the precursor of the contemporary figural shaker. To hold condiments was obviously the lesser function of this lavish conversation piece. Because salt originates in the sea, and pepper on land, Cellini placed a boat-shaped salt container under the guardianship of Neptune, while the pepper is watched over by a personification of Earth.

The first commercial salt and pepper shakers were manufactured in England during the 1860s. Made of glass and fine china, these sets reflect Victorian design sensibilities. The first patent for a novelty shaker was recorded in 1909, and by the mid-1920s figural and novelty shakers were being manufactured by the thousands both here and abroad.

As collectibles, salt and pepper shakers are becoming increasingly valuable. It is ironic, in fact, that the price of containers for salt and pepper has outstripped the cost of the seasonings themselves. There was a time when salt was used as currency, and when entire continents depended on the salt trade for their economic well-being. Today, salt and pepper are commonplace, while the shakers that hold them are becoming increasingly rare and have started to command hefty prices.

This book is concerned primarily with figural and novelty sets manufactured in Japan, Europe, and the United States since the 1920s. Ranging in size from one-half inch to several feet, the shakers in this volume are tributes to transportation and technology, gastronomy and music, human rituals and the wild kingdom. I have tried to choose sets that appeal to the messy vitality of the popular imagination, that collective vision that runs the gamut from Walt Disney to Westinghouse. As the book evolved, Miriam Seger, my photographic collaborator, and I felt that photographs of shakers should explore options beyond those established for collectible art. To this end, we constructed elaborate dioramas and used shakers as a cast of characters to tell theme-oriented stories. Finally, a warning: collecting shakers can be habit-forming.

1

Paradise Found

Easy to pack and not too pricey, shakers of landmark attractions helped fulfill the desire of the peregrinating masses to bring alien and exotic things closer to home

Highly treasured and difficult to find is an exquisitely painted metal set made in the early 1950s by M. S. Products, in which two river boats (salt and pepper) are set on a tray cast in the shape of Niagara Falls.

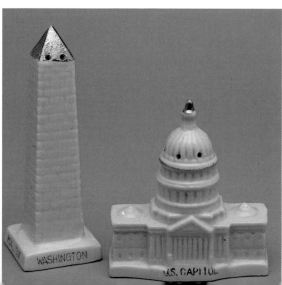

Paradise Found

Although the first novelty shaker was patented near the turn of the century, production of such sets took a quantum leap in the 1940s and 1950s when American families loaded tots, pets, and food rations into woodies or ragtops and set off on blue highway adventures across the country. Easy to pack and not too pricey, shakers of landmark attractions, from the Empire State Building and Niagara Falls to Mt. Rushmore and the Space Needle, not only recorded visits to famous spots—they made it possible for the average American to relish those picturesque landscapes and monuments at home. Hot pink flamingoes from the San Diego Zoo, ferocious plastic alligators from the Florida Everglades, and two-piece ceramic volcanoes glazed with ash from Mt. St. Helens reflect American consciousness in a self-important and acquisitive mood.

Glorifying famous places and landmarks—while, at the same time, subduing and miniaturizing them—salt and pepper shakers made it possible for collectors to continue to share in the power and majesty of what they had seen. More than any other tourist artifact, except perhaps the picture postcard, shakers helped fulfill the desire of the peregrinating masses to bring alien and exotic things close to home.

Salt and pepper mania, cross-country style, knew no limits. Empire State Building and Statue of Liberty sets that proliferated during the late 1940s and early 1950s made it possible for salt and pepper aficionados to leap tall buildings in a single bound and, what's more, shake the living daylights out of them with the impunity of Superman. Three-piece metal sets in which these landmarks sit on a rose-decorated tray are among the finest in this series. But the most prized in this architectural lineage is a single-piece bronze set in which the Statue of Liberty and Empire State Building rise triumphantly from a stepped-back base modeled after the New York City skyline.

After the Empire State Building and Statue of Liberty, Niagara Falls generated more varieties of shakers than any other tourist landmark. Owners of one wacky three-piece ceramic set can blithely pluck one half of Niagara Falls from its scenic base and sprinkle salt over their scrambled eggs, and then pick up the other half of the falls to add a pinch of pepper. Other humorous ceramic shakers depict Alcatraz prisoners and plastic camels whose humps are used for spice storage.

The souvenir shaker offers a nearly limitless repertoire of representations. By the late 1950s, there were enough shakers around to bury the avid collector in an avalanche of artifactual marginalia and visual ephemera. With a selection ranging from Alaskan igloos and Mormon temples to Japanese pagodas and the Washington Monument, the burgeoning desire to collect salt and pepper memorabilia seemed every bit as urgent as the accompanying penchant to supplant every reality with a reproduction.

Available in blue/orange and black/white color schemes, slick two-tone plastic shakers of the Trylon and Perisphere were produced by the Emeloid Company of Arlington, New Jersey, for the 1939 World's Fair.

Ivory shakers carved with Italy's architectural masterpieces are extremely rare, as are these pot metal shakers of the state of Arizona. Florida vacation spots commissioned many whimsical shakers such as the one-piece alligator set. The souvenir windmills from San Francisco are covered in leather.

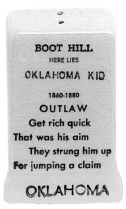

Plastic, metal, and ceramic versions of the Seattle Space Needle were manufactured in the late 1960s. Painted polychrome shakers made from pot metal, like this dazzling San Diego set, are among the most sought-after souvenir shakers.

 OREGON   BEAVER STATE

FLORIDA   FLORIDA

A novel mix 'n' match strategy prevails in the design of a two-piece Florida set displaying graceful flamingoes and black-laced angelfish inside water-filled snowdomes. Designed by the Parksmith Company of New York, and made in Hong Kong, these shakers are rigged with chambers holding salt and pepper.

P 7734 ALCATRAZ   S 7734 ALCATRAZ

MARINELAND   MARINELAND

San Francisco 1952

Greetings from MISSOURI

2

Leave the Driving to Us

As early as the 1940s, shaker design began to reflect America's love affair with movement and exploration

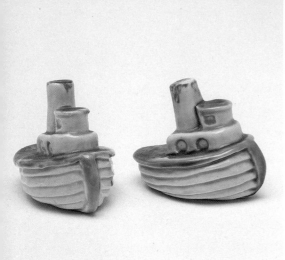

Leave the Driving to Us

"Today, speed is the cry of our era," wrote American designer Norman Bel Geddes in 1932, "and even greater speed one of the goals of tomorrow." Though living in the darkest days of the Depression, Bel Geddes, like other Americans, was looking ahead to safe, fast travel on luxurious streamlined aircraft, trains, buses, ships, and automobiles. His prediction proved to be visionary. For more than half a century, America's love affair with movement and exploration has verged on the obsessive, confirming Norman Mailer's claim that "travel is the great American disease."

As early as the 1940s, shaker design began to reflect a growing enchantment with vehicles, especially automobiles. A limited edition of roadster shakers painted in 22-karat gold appeared in the late 1940s; in the 1950s shakers took the form of miniature Chrysler Airflow automobiles with adjoining Airstream trailers, plastic Model T Fords (the driver and passenger were salt and pepper vessels), and other racing cars modeled after Mercedes-Benz and Indianapolis prototypes. Most car shakers were made of ceramic and many had movable metal wheels. Some vehicles were fashioned after lumber trucks, tricycles, and sportscars. A ceramic set consisting of a flat tire and air pump captured the pitfalls of cross-country travel, while the accompaniments of highway cruising ap-

peared in the form of traffic lights, snow tires, and plastic gasoline pumps.

Gasoline stations and fast-food restaurants have been the traditional gathering places for an American culture obsessed with life on the road. Like church spires piercing the sky, the Flying Pegasus of Mobilgas, fluorescent-lit Dairy Queen cones, and fire helmets advertising Sky Chief gasoline became immutable fixtures of America's middle-class landscape that charted the way through main drags across the land. During the 1940s and 1950s, shakers bearing paper stickers indicating gasoline prices in the 30-cent-per-gallon range were produced in the form of plastic gas pumps imprinted with such names as Esso, Gulf, Mobilgas, Richfield, Phillips 66, Amoco, Sky Chief, Amlico, or Conoco, and given to customers as gifts or premiums.

America's love affair with wide open spaces was celebrated by the Greyhound Bus Company in the early 1940s, when it commissioned a novelty company to manufacture pot metal buses, complete with movable rubber wheels. Originally available at tourist outposts, the two-axle, six-wheel single-decker bus is a particularly handsome shaker, highlighting the sensuous curves and streamlining that characterized industrial design of the Depression Modern period. Boasting three miniature axles and ten

tires, matching pairs of double-decker shaker Scenicruisers appeared in the 1960s. The painting technique used for Greyhound shakers was inferior, and mint sets, when available, command premium prices.

The Firestone Tire and Rubber Company also capitalized on the magic of wheels in motion with the production of a pair of shakers depicting thick-treaded snow tires.

The association of shakers and means of transport took many forms. Bronze steam engines and ceramic locomotives paired with coal cars and cabooses evoke memories of old Number 9 chugging along the mountainside or the Twentieth-Century Limited streaking across a vast continent. The allure of river-cruising and transoceanic travel was honored with exotic shakers designed in the shape of gondolas, schooners, oceanliners, and tugboats with salt and pepper chambers concealed in the smokestacks. Exquisite hand-painted tugboats and oceanliners made in Occupied Japan between 1945 and 1952 are among the finest sets manufactured during this era.

Not surprisingly, the war effort of the 1940s encouraged production of military transport and fighter vehicles, among them crashing Air Force bombers, tanks, and rockets, many sculpted from chalk and painted by hand.

During the 1950s and 1960s, the

Heather House of Burlington, Iowa, responded to America's cross-country travel craze with mail-order sales of ceramic shakers consisting of states (salt) and their symbols (pepper). Manufactured by Park Craft and available for $1.25 a pair through the Heather House catalog, each of the states, including Alaska and Hawaii, was paired with an appropriate icon, foodstuff, or commercial product. Michigan is paired with a sleek blue-green sedan, Illinois with a bust of Abraham Lincoln, and Connecticut with a mortarboard marked "Yale." North Carolina is paired with a pack of cigarettes, New Jersey with Miss America, and New Mexico with an Indian Pueblo. Although the states are grossly out of scale with one another, it is possible to assemble an idiosyncratic map of the United States with pieces from the Heather House collection.

Greyhound Scenicruiser buses, complete with movable rubber wheels, were available as premiums beginning in the late 1930s. The streamlined Airstream trailers reflect design trends that were popular during the Depression Modern period. Polystyrene shakers illustrate the rocket mania of the early 1950s.

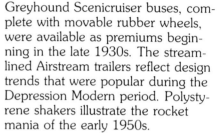

This San Francisco cable car prepares for a track switch. A turn-of-the-century tricycle stores condiments in glass shakers. Ground artillery and "victory" bombs were made of chalk during the late 1940s.

3

Home on the Range

Cowboy and Indian shakers lean toward typical Western scenes: gun-toting buckaroos with their faithful palominos, showdowns between masked desperadoes, and American Indians in traditional attire

Favored for their rich details and vibrant pigments, cowboy and Indian shakers run the gamut from the zany and endearing to the ritualistic.

Home on the Range

Beginning in the 1930s, tourist centers west of the Mississippi began to experience a brisk business in the salt and pepper trade. Indian councils in New Mexico and Arizona produced a potpourri of Indian-related sets, while tourist vendors in Montana, Colorado, and Nevada distributed shakers illustrating nearly every facet of cowboy life from Tony Lama boots to bucking buckaroos. The most meticulously crafted shakers in this genre were hand-painted ceramic and chalk sets depicting native American Indians in elaborate headdresses, facial paint, and traditional attire. Teepees, canoes,

moccasins, and totem poles were popular ''go-withs'' and drew heavily on local color schemes and geometric patterns. Indian head shakers made from a wood composite were popular in the 1940s, while the 1950s saw a flood of pot metal shakers. Indian craftsmen edged shaker design into new territory by using cowhide, horse hair, and beads on sets shaped like drums, and putting hand-tinted feathers atop shakers of Indian chiefs and squaws.

Cowboy shakers lean toward stereotypical Western scenarios: gun-toting John Wayne lookalikes with their faithful palominos, showdowns between masked despera-

does, and bucking horses ridden by Lone Ranger types. The Death Valley landscape of shakers is peppered with bleached cattle skulls, prickly pear cacti, and rattlesnakes. Except for cowboy boot shakers made of Bakelite, and a few delicately painted porcelain figures, nearly all Wild West sets are hand-painted ceramic. The most collectible are two-piece sets with a rider atop a rearing horse. Made in the 1950s and featuring a young, rosy-cheeked cowpoke glued to his horse, these sets evoke the heart-plucking television show ''Fury''— ''The story of a horse and the boy who loved him.''

The animal skin and colored beads on the Indian drum shakers give an impression of authenticity. Grazing animals and saddle horses are also popular Wild West subjects.

Made in Mexico, wooden stage-coaches painted with bright pigments highlight salt and pepper vessels. Colorful headdresses decorate Indian shakers, while bucking horses in metal and ceramic celebrate the rough and tumble rodeo theme.

CHUCK WAGON

4

Counter Culture

Combining delicate craftsmanship and narrative bite, fruit and vegetable shakers hit on a recipe that is held in high esteem by collectors

Cherries are made of red Carrara glass and lead. Porcelain pineapples sparkle with 22-karat gold paint highlights. Watermelons and metal-topped beer shakers are available in several varieties.

A worm in the apple will probably not keep the doctor away. Chalk sets of freshwater trout and ceramic shakers of pie à la mode reflect the vast assortment of food shakers.

Counter Culture

Between the 1930s and 1960s, shaker manufacturers paid tribute to America's rich and bountiful harvests with ceramic and porcelain shakers depicting nearly every comestible under the sun. Corn, lamb chops, and baked potatoes (usually with a pat of butter) were common staples in the salt and pepper trade of the 1940s and 1950s. As the economy ripened and American fruit farms blossomed in California and Florida during the late 1950s, succulent fare such as Macintosh apples (including worm-infested specimens), Hawaiian pineapples, and watermelons, were adapted to the world of shakers. And several years before the rage for vegetarianism, matching two-piece sets of asparagus, zucchini, cabbage, beans, and other "rabbit food" had sprouted in the shaker market.

Nibbling away at the sprout and tofu movement of the 1960s was that old American appetite for grease, sugar, and red meat. Attuned to the gastronomic offerings of well-oiled cooking conglomerates, movers and shakers in the salt and pepper trade began to cook up sets that venerated hamburgers, hot dogs, cupcakes, Dairy Queen cones, pie à la mode, and other cholesterol-laden snacks.

Food shakers would have been just another bland category if not for the "fruit and vegetable people," a deliciously painted family of anthropomorphic shakers with human bodies grafted to stylized fruit and vegetable faces. Designed by National Potteries Company (NAPCO) of Cleveland, Ohio, and manufactured between 1930 and 1945, these ceramic sets feature a wide range of storybook characters

with superb detailing and coloring. Sets with gold-painted lace trim are almost always made of porcelain.

A later vintage of produce row shakers boasting oversized cartoon faces appeared during the 1940s and 1950s. Pushing the anthropomorphic theme to its fermentation point, these lyrical sets feature fully attired fruit and vegetable characters engaged in some of life's more intoxicating pastimes: swinging baseball bats, playing violins, and dancing the night away. With heads in appetizing combinations— watermelons with cantaloupes, tomatoes with peppers, carrots with onions, oranges with lemons—fruit and vegetable shakers hit on a recipe which combines delicate craftsmanship with narrative bite and is still held in high esteem by collectors of fine shakers.

Shakers cater to America's fondness for gooey ice cream sundaes and the more wholesome fare of corn and baked potatoes.

Apple and orange lift out of this fruit basket to dispense salt and pepper. The eggplant twins (fig friends?) are part of a large and zany family of fruit and vegetable people.

5

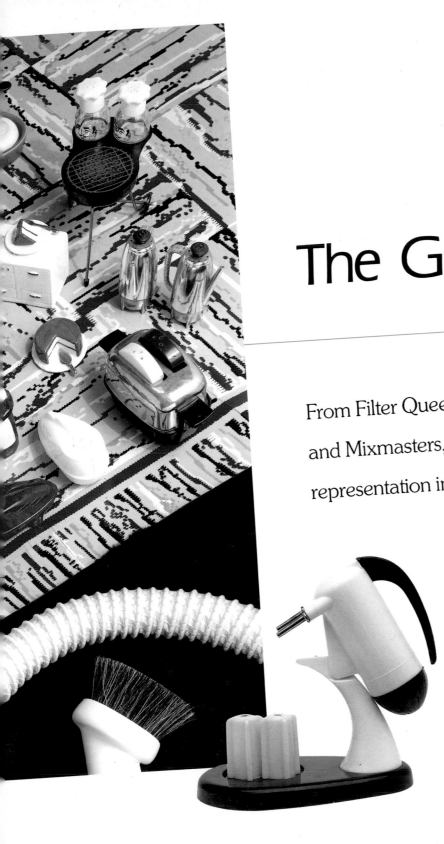

The Good Life

From Filter Queens and barbecue grills to Osterizers and Mixmasters, few modern appliances escaped representation in shaker form

The Art Deco set at lower left is made from stainless steel and plastic. The miniature power lawn mower has movable wheels; its white condiment containers move up and down like pistons. Plastic valet shakers were manufactured with garments painted in various colors.

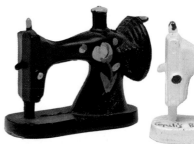

The Good Life

Salt and pepper shakers manufactured during the 1950s were designed for an America buoyed by postwar optimism and soothed by the tranquility of the Eisenhower years; their appeal was pitched to a culture hypnotized by the televised bliss of Ozzie and Harriet and fascinated by labor-saving devices that symbolized the good life just around the corner. From Filter Queens and Weber barbecue grills to Osterizers and Mixmasters, few modern appliances escaped representation in shaker form. Ceramic shakers of this era paid tribute to the teeny-weeny yellow polka dot bikini (in his 'n' hers styles) and other trendy fashions, while plastic shakers featuring mechanical parts honored cars with tailfins, Airstream trailers, and other symbols of the American Dream.

The 1950s also saw a baroque flowering in popular entertainment, especially rock 'n' roll music. Shakers fashioned in the shape of guitars, electric pianos, and TV consoles reflect the meteoric rise in the latest popular music and home entertainment media. Even one of the country's premier ceramic makers, the Lenox China Company, contributed to this new wave with a matching set picturing Nipper the Dog, the trademark for the Radio Corporation of America.

Boxed sets stamped "Occupied Japan" and plastic shakers with movable mechanical parts are among the period's more novel—and highly prized—offerings. Made of opaque glass and available in colors such as amber, cobalt blue, and amethyst, light bulb shakers produced in Japan for Chadwick-Miller, Inc., of Boston, were packaged, as might be expected, in sleeves of corrugated cardboard. On occasion, packaging design took on a mystique of its own and fueled America's infatuation with leisure living. An elaborate multicolored box labeled "Penthouse Salt & Pepper" displays two plastic coffee pot shakers on a balcony framed by a three-dimensional cutout of a striped canopy and New York City's glittering nocturnal skyline. Made by Brillium Metals Corporation of Long Island, the back of this elaborate package bears the following inscription: "The excitement of Penthouse living, the glamour of dinner at The Ritz will be yours when you add these authentic miniatures to your table setting." Salt and pepper power at its most decadent.

Functional modernism, mid-century style, dramatically influenced shaker design and encouraged production of sets that reflected the forms and rituals of the age—efficiency, flowing curves, and a minimum of distraction. The more ingenious machine age shakers unobtrusively incorporate—or better yet, conceal—salt and pepper vessels within the overall design of the miniaturized object. Frequently, spice chambers are so cleverly hidden that finding them becomes somewhat of a challenge for the uninitiated collector. Zaniness in shaker design broke new ground with the "Tiny Power Lawn Mower." Manufactured in both red and brown plastic versions, the mower shaker conceals its bounty inside two plastic cylinders—one for salt and the other for pepper—that move up and down like pistons.

Whether hokey or hilarious, shakers of the 1950s venerated, above all, labor-saving appliances that began to pepper the domestic landscape. Slick and streamlined, a miniature Hamilton Beach mixer houses the flavor-enhancing duo in each of its corked beaters, reserving the removable bowl for sugar. Pop-up toasters (the burnt brown "slice" is for pepper and the white slice is for salt), L'il Washer (the wringers, where else?), and upright pianos that extrude shakers at the top when the keys are pressed, round out the fabulous '50s and its fascination with things movable and modern.

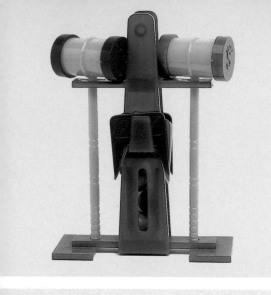

By 1959, it was possible to outfit an entire dollhouse kitchen and home with miniature appliances and furnishings filled with salt and pepper.

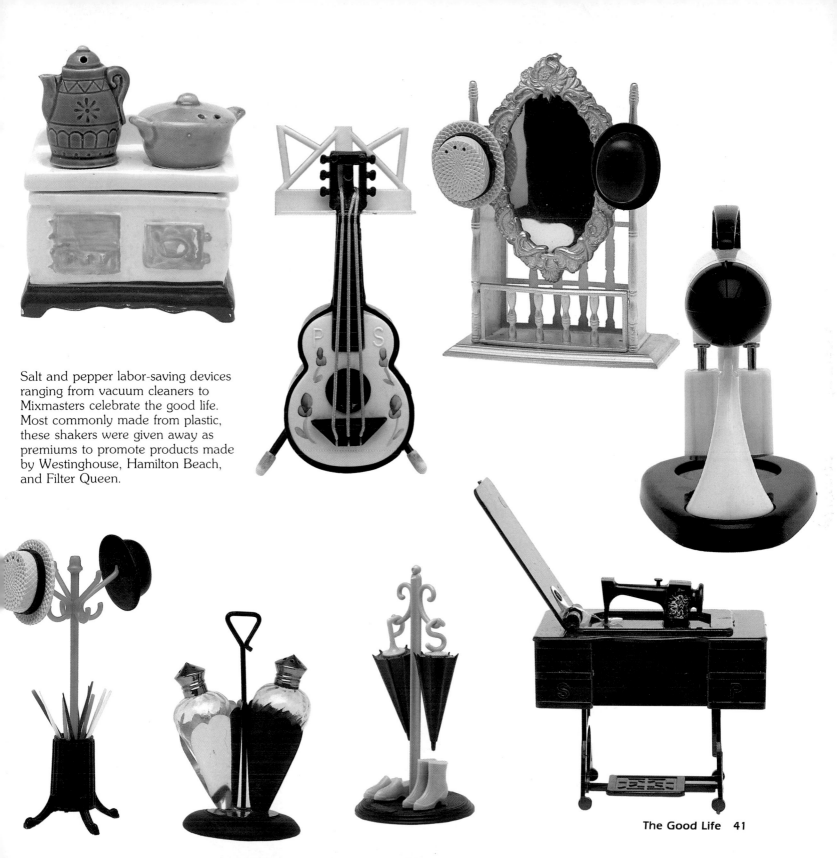

Salt and pepper labor-saving devices ranging from vacuum cleaners to Mixmasters celebrate the good life. Most commonly made from plastic, these shakers were given away as premiums to promote products made by Westinghouse, Hamilton Beach, and Filter Queen.

6

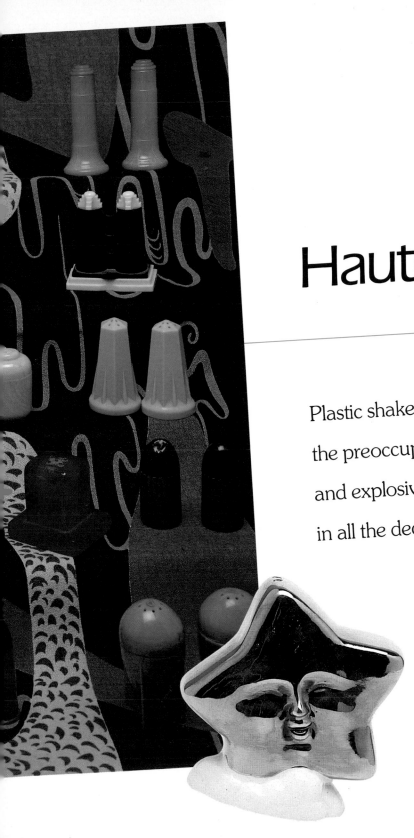

Haute Shakeur

Plastic shakers of the 1930s and 1940s reflect
the preoccupation with bold colors, crystalline forms,
and explosive geometrics that influenced design
in all the decorative arts

Salt and pepper meet the Machine Age in a nut and bolt set made of acrylic. Metal swan features movable wings, while plastic shakers are decorated with paper-thin rose petals. Oyster shaker flips open to reveal two pearl-like containers.

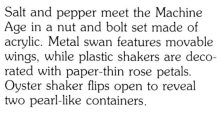

Haute Shakeur

Although shakers depicting motorized symbols of the good life reached their zenith in the 1950s, a preoccupation with the crystalline forms of the Machine Age and the decorative energy of Art Deco had begun to influence shaker design as early as the 1930s. This was an era in which shakers were designed for design's sake. From the brightly colored plasticware boasting skyscraper-like stepbacks to miniature pastel-colored sets with smooth, sensuous curves, shakers of the 1930s and 1940s reflect the polychrome flashiness and explosive geometrics that influenced design in all the decorative arts. Not surprisingly, these shakers have gained in popularity and, like other Art Deco collectibles, have begun to command premium prices.

Among the most desirable sets are those made of Bakelite (the trade name for the first synthetic industrial plastic invented in 1909) a tough thermosetting phenolic resin known as "the material of a thousand uses." Manufactured almost entirely in America by the Burroughs Co., Daka-Ware, Carvanite, and many other companies, these two-piece sets were produced in hundreds of colors, both translucent and opaque. Those shakers featuring smooth marbleized finishes are the most collectible of this group, which is characterized by thick, heavy walls and miniscule chambers for salt and pepper.

A pair of obelisk shakers, souvenirs from the Washington Monument, as well as other spire-like sets made of cast phenolic resin in retina-searing colors reflect shaker design from this period at its finest. Produced in several delicious shades of aquamarine, blue-green, and yellow-orange, many of the sets made in the 1930s and 1940s project the style and elegance more likely encountered in an Eric von Stroheim film than in the family kitchen.

Despite the "uptown" aura of shakers made from cast phenolic resin, polystyrene-based plastics became the rage for novelty shakers introduced in the late 1940s. During World War II, plastic sets shaped like shotgun shells were even used as advertisements for ammunition companies. One of the most popular shakers of this vintage is activated by a small dispensing button beneath the base. When pushed, a small plastic piece lifts off like a rocket from the top of the shaker and releases the spice for a real charge.

Acrylic resins gained wide commercial use in the late 1940s and their versatility made it possible to design a family of shakers that drew on the latest in machine shop technology. In these sets, salt and pepper chambers were bored out of clear one-inch thick acrylic slabs and then connected to small exit conduits drilled from the exterior. The result is a stark and sleek miniaturized monolith that looks better suited for storing motor oil than salt and pepper. Eventually, the industrial image of these one-piece acrylic sets was softened by plastic floral and fish motifs embedded into the clear plastic. Among the most appealing acrylic shakers are two-piece sets based on bold horizontal geometrics in which colored opaque and clear acrylic components alternate along a vertical spice-filled metal shaft.

This plastic goose set lays two golden eggs of salt and pepper. Plastic, wood veneer, and silica inlay are used to create elegant geometric patterns in the set at far left. Rock fragments, sea shells, and crystals give souvenir shakers an oceanside aura. Plastic clothespin shaker and metal toothpaste tube push shakerware into the realm of the surreal.

7

Wild Kingdom

The topsy-turvy world of animal shakers is best described in a phrase: "It's a jungle out there"

Realistic marsh birds and other wild-fowl are among the exquisite hand-painted ceramic sets made by Osuga in Japan during the late 1940s.

Wild Kingdom

Although plastic shakers boasting bold patterns and vivid colors enjoyed enormous popularity during their heyday in the 1930s and 1940s, they never supplanted the appeal of figural shakers made from ceramic and porcelain. Shakers depicting wild flora and fauna have been popular since the 1920s, and are still being produced today.

The topsy-turvy world of wild and woolly shakers is best described in a single phrase: "It's a jungle out there." And a steamy one at that. Many collectors find that a single pair of animal shakers has the uncanny ability to breed, and before long their shelves are overrun with a vast ceramic menagerie. From green-headed mallards and iridescent angelfish to cuddly farm animals and grisly-faced reptiles of the Jurassic period, the call of the wild inspired production of a wide-branching family tree of salt and peppers, both in the United States and abroad.

The most eclectic group of all shaker types, the "table-top zoo" consists of sets made from bone china, porcelain, chalk, and metal. Some of the more elaborate hand-painted sets evoke the work of well-known visual artists. A number of bird shakers manufactured during the late 1940s are reminiscent of illustrations by John James Audubon, while in the flower family subtly tinted ceramic sets of calla lilies evoke the paintings of Georgia O'Keeffe, and shakers of horses twisting in romantic agony are reminiscent of the work of Eugène Delacroix.

The William Goebbel Company of Germany, known for its Hummel figures, designed and manufactured several animal shakers between 1940 and 1956. A number of fine animal bisque pieces—many modeled on work by European companies such as Belleek and Goebbel—were made in Japan between 1950 and 1952. Osuga Ware pieces are, perhaps, the finest Japanese creations in this category. However, American contributions to the animal kingdom are among the most imaginative. The Ceramic Arts Studio of Madison, Wisconsin, and the Whapeton Pottery Company (Rosemade) of North Dakota—the country's most prolific producers of animal shakers—gained a reputation for exquisitely painted and delicately crafted salt and peppers, many of them glazed with bright pigments faithful to species coloration. Hand-painted fish shakers with the species name printed on the bottom satisfied the curiosity of would-be naturalists.

Designers working with animal characters produced a number of ingenious shaker types, including "carriers," "huggers," "nesters," "nodders," and "hangers," to portray the complex world of animal behavior. Made from a number of materials, including glazed ceramic, reinforced felt, and red clay, three-piece animal carriers include sets in which beasts of burden—donkeys, pink elephants, and purple cows—carry salt and pepper vessels crafted to look like baskets, barrels, and milk cans.

Monkeys swinging on trees and birds perched on branches are popular shaker themes for "hangers," sets in which salt and pepper holders hang precariously from a common base. "Nesters" are two- and three-piece sets in which either one part rests on the other, or two pieces are nestled into a common base. Monkeys clutching bananas, mice nestled into wedges of Swiss cheese, acorn-toting squirrels, and bears holding salmon are among the most colorful and popular entries in this category. "Huggers" refer to two-piece sets in which salt and pepper fragments are joined together to create the appearance of a single shaker. Common examples of this type are horses wrapped around hay bundles, puppies embracing garbage cans, and two-piece sets in which animals are split into anterior and posterior sections. Bird heads and skulls are favored motifs for "nodders," three-piece sets in which salt and pepper chambers with long necks are fitted into notches on a base and then set into a rocking motion. Lowest on the great chain of shaker beings are wooden "squeaker" sets, which produce strange animal noises when turned upside down.

"Carriers" usually depict donkeys saddled with cargo, while "hangers" feature monkeys, bears, and birds clutching or swinging from branches. Kangaroo shakers are among the most popular in the "nester" group.

Fish and birds are favored for "nodders," three-piece ceramic sets in which salt and pepper chambers with long necks are balanced on notches and then set into motion.

The Ceramic Arts Studio of Madison, Wisconsin, and Whapeton Pottery Company (Rosemade) of North Dakota, specialized in high-quality, hand-painted ceramic shakers that describe many kinds of animal behavior.

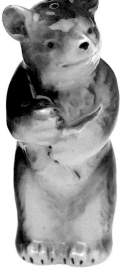

Interlocking necks add a humorous twist to the giraffe shakers, while action and movement are suggested in the posture of the swordfish shakers. The trio of monkeys, See No Evil, Hear No Evil, and Speak No Evil, are also in salt and pepper form.

8

Animal Farm

Man's anthropomorphic tendencies are admirably expressed in shakers of guitar-playing penguins and pigs gussied up to look like divas

Animal Farm

Man's anthropomorphic tendencies are admirably expressed in shakers of donkeys wailing on saxophones, guitar-playing penguins, and pigs gussied up to look like divas. Owls in graduation garb sporting pink sunglasses over inset rhinestone eyes bring this humanizing impulse into the realm of the bizarre. Nearly all sets in this group are made of ceramic and many are hand-painted. The most elaborate and fantastic pieces—duck accordion players and pianists from the mouse family—were made in Japan between 1945 and April 28, 1952, and are stamped "Occupied Japan" on the bottom.

The pig is considered the most collectible of all farm animals. Some of the most durable and sought-after sets were manufactured between 1937 and 1961 by the Shawnee Pottery Company of Zanesville, Ohio. Adorable humanoid faces, paper labels bearing the company's imprint, and large openings on the bottom of the shakers help identify Shawnee sets, which feature a distinctive white glossy glaze punctuated by spare detailing in primary colors. Matching cookie jars and other kitchen items accompanied the extensive line of Shawnee shakers. Unlike pigs and cartoon animals made by Shawnee's competitor, the American Pottery Company (A.P.Co.) of Marietta, Ohio, Shawnee shakers were always painted *beneath* the glaze, making them especially durable and resistant to chipping. Shawnee shakers trimmed with 22-karat gold paint are very much in demand and command premium prices. The German-born ceramicist Rudy Ganz was Shawnee's first designer and worked for the company between 1939 and 1954. He designed the Puss 'N Boots, Mugsy Dog, Little Bo Peep, and Boy Pig and Farmer sets produced during the mid-1940s.

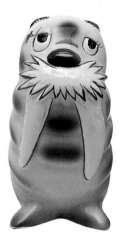

9

Salt of the Earth

With rich glazes applied to ceramic or
porcelain, figural shakers confirm the old adage,
"variety is the spice of life"

Salt of the Earth

The diverse world of shakers is peppered with men and women for all seasons, confirming the old adage, "variety is the spice of life." Displaying rich glazes applied to ceramic and porcelain, figural shakers portray a spectrum of cultural types from dancing hula girls and kissing Eskimos to Oriental rice farmers and American spacemen. During the late 1960s, even flower children attired in necklaces with peace signs and President John F. Kennedy sitting in his rocking chair were portrayed in salt and pepper. Between 1920 and the late 1950s, Japanese manufacturers successfully imitated shaker styles of several European companies, including Goebbel, and Holland's delftware, with its sets of kissing boys and girls and other Dutch figures in native dress.

Shakers depicting stereotypical images of racial inferiority represent a blighted period in the history of salt and pepper. However, figural black shakers are among the most beautifully made. Shakers featuring Africans in native dress and jewelry were often hand-trimmed in 22-karat gold paint before glazing. Because molds were often traded between manufacturers, it is common to see sets that are identical save for color and decoration. The Ceramic Art Studios of Madison, Wisconsin, and the Pearl China Company of Cleveland, Ohio, produced the most complete and imaginative lines of black salt and pepper memorabilia. Many sets featured black characters who had become symbols for major American food companies—Aunt Jemima for General Mills, Tappan Chefs for Tappan Range, Uncle Rastus for Cream of Wheat, and Luzianne Mammy for the now-defunct Luzianne Coffee Company. Because shakers of "black Americana" have not been produced for almost three decades, they command premium prices and, not surprisingly, are extremely difficult to find.

A quirky, often cynical, humorous streak can be detected in many "two-sided" figural shakers. In one popular set, the "before" side depicts a svelte young couple aglow in marital bliss; the "after" side reveals a husband with an exaggerated paunch and a pregnant wife. In another "two-sided" shaker, the "before" couple is upbeat and cheerful, while the "after" side shows them in the middle of an altercation, their hand-painted faces contorted with rage. Reflecting the more upbeat side of domestic life are the "bench people." In these large sets, especially popular during the 1950s and 1960s, two ceramic pieces of a kissing or embracing couple sit atop a wooden bench.

Shakers of black Americana reflect outdated racial stereotypes. Beginning in the 1950s, the Aunt Jemima and Uncle Mose set spearheaded the Quaker Oats pancake mix campaign. These brightly colored sets were available to the public as a premium in exchange for boxtops. Produced in both short (3½″) and tall (5½″) varieties, these sets were part of a group of Aunt Jemima giveaways made by the F&F Mold and Die Works.

Spacemen shakers are 1960s vintage. Milliner with hatboxes and Oriental man with watering baskets reflect the fine craftsmanship of hand-painted sets made in Occupied Japan during the late 1940s and early 1950s.

Figural shakers of the human melting pot portray a broad spectrum of cultural types and occupations.

10

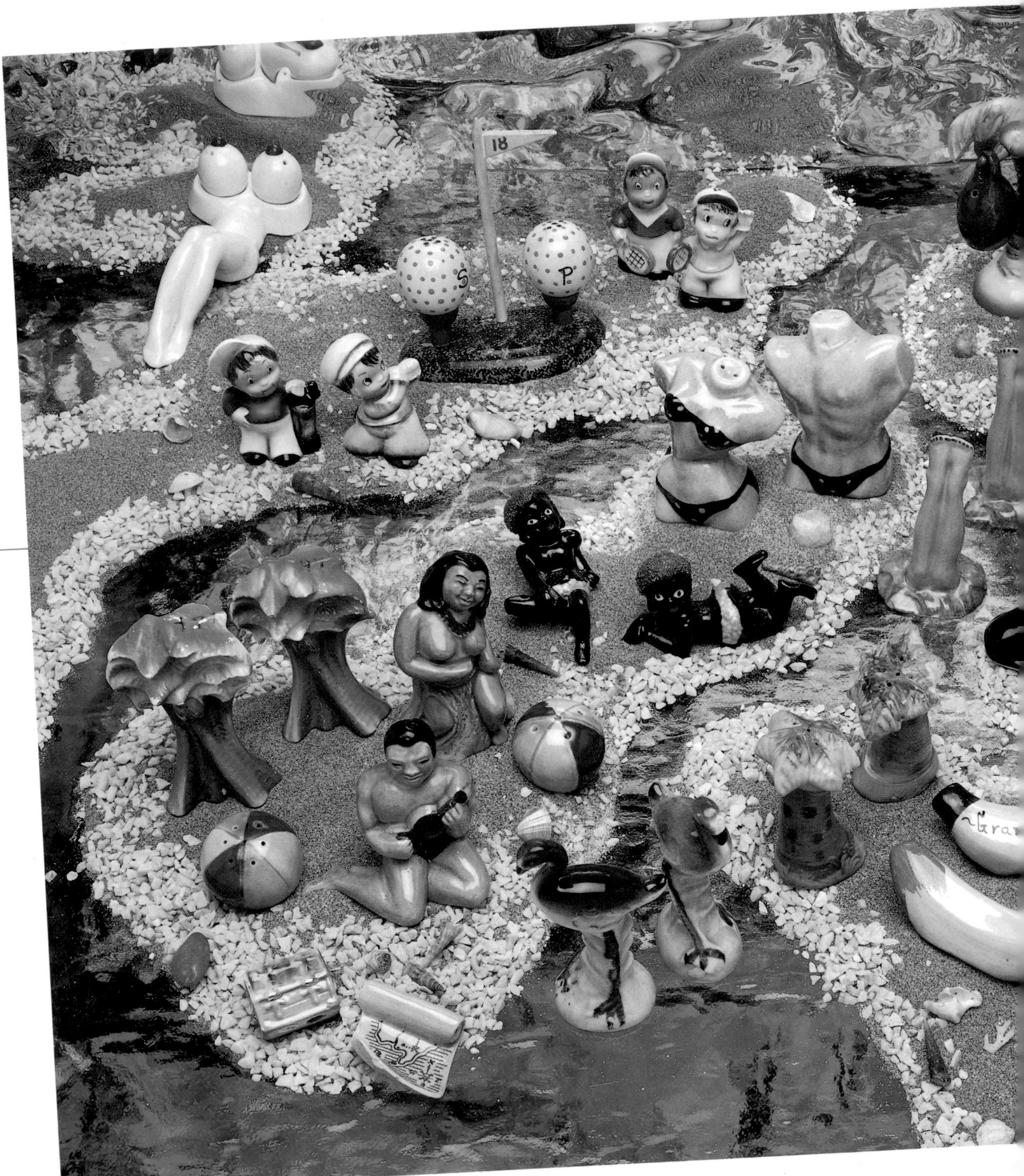

Name Your Game

From pugilists and putters to canoeists and coxswains, figural shakers articulate the thrill of victory and the agony of defeat

Pugilist shakers are characterized by exaggerated face-offs and flailing limbs. The excitement of the bullfight and the more conventional American sports of golf, bowling, and canoeing are well represented by shakers.

Name Your Game

Sports are admirably represented in the world of salt and pepper. Bat-wielding heroes of the diamond, aficionados of the left hook, and speedskating puckmasters are only a few of the athletes celebrated in shaker form. From pugilists and putters to canoeists and coxswains, figural shakers have successfully articulated the thrill of victory and the agony of defeat. Only a few articles of athletic gear have escaped miniaturization in shaker form. Wooden bowling balls, ceramic baseballs and footballs, and metal cricket bats (made in England) are some of the shakers found on the shelf of the discriminating collector. A number of unusual shakers pay tribute to such offbeat sports as deep-sea diving, bullfighting, and sumo wrestling.

Most sports-related sets were made in Japan between 1940 and the present. The finer shakers are hand-painted beneath a glossy glaze; however, chalk-like ceramic sets hand-painted with a matte finish also are common. Of all the athletes revered in shaker land, pugilists boast the most expressive poses and facial details. Hand-painted ceramic sets made during the late 1940s and early 1950s depict clashing titans with beefy slabs of muscle, grimacing faces, and flailing limbs ready to deliver a smoking blue gumball.

Many salt and peppers capture the mood of the competitors and combatants they portray. Baseball lore, especially, was a powerful inspiration for designers and elevated craft humor to new shaker heights. Grumpy hitters are paired with defiant umpires, while pitchers are shown snarling at opposing batters.

11

Pouring
Cats and Dogs

Cat and dog shakers explore humorous themes

associated with this faithful domestic duo

Colorful and expressive, ceramic shakers of cats and dogs run the gamut from complementary pairs to identical twins to playful pets.

Pouring Cats and Dogs

Whether realistic, expressionistic, or cartoon-like, cat and dog shakers explore just about every humorous theme associated with this faithful domestic duo, ranging from dogs wrapped around fire hydrants to cats perched atop eight balls to schnauzers peering out of hats. In the 1950s, a line of black cat kitchenware, including salt and pepper shakers, was very popular. Called Shafford pottery, these pieces feature high gloss black glaze applied to a red clay base. Distinguished by fire engine red ears and bow ties, Shafford black cats were made in all shapes and sizes, including a long (12 inches) and bizarre one-piece set with a cork on each end. One of the quirkier cat pairs is a two-piece set made from painted magnets and cat hair whiskers.

Dalmatians, dachshunds, and gingham dogs (with calico cats) are popular breeds in the shaker canine corps. French poodles are sometimes trimmed with "gingerbread" to create thick curly collars and coiffures. Although the overwhelming majority of cat and dog shakers are made from ceramic, a number of garishly painted chalkware sets were manufactured between 1920 and the early 1950s by the Pennsylvania Dutch community. While the spectrum of cat and dog chalkware is quite interesting, it is difficult to find sets from this material in good condition.

Black cat shakers are actually painted magnets. The "nester" with two dogs in a wagon and other canine caricatures are among the more unusual entries in the dog category.

Mother and puppy sets are common among canine shakers. Other frequently seen pairs are cats and dogs engaged in playful antics.

12

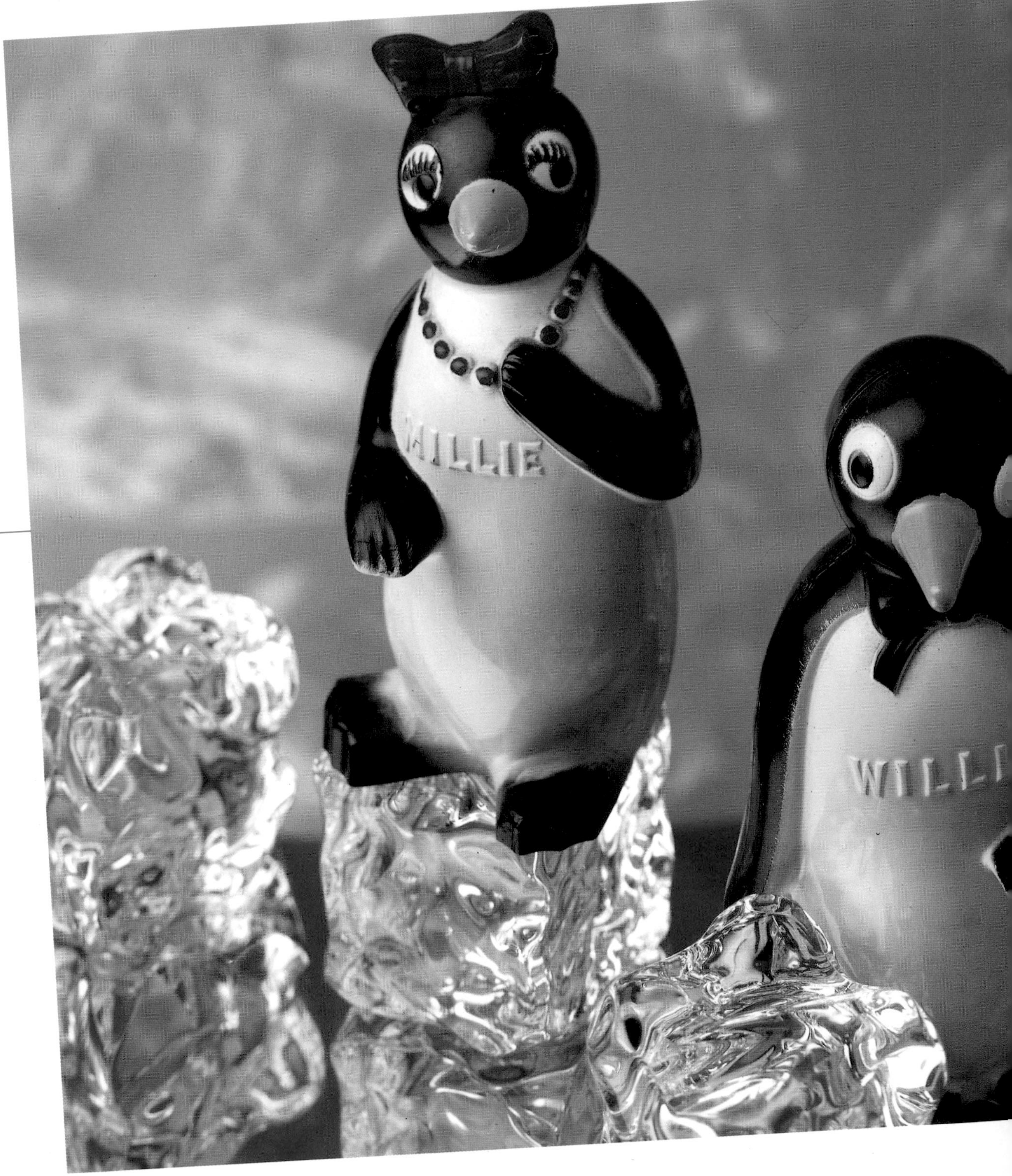

Celebrity Shakes

The quirky vitality of American entrepreneurship expresses itself in shakers promoting products from peanuts and flour mixes to cigarettes and dog food

Heroes including Dick Tracy, Jonah and the Whale, Little Red Riding Hood and the Wolf, and others add a touch of fantasy to salt and pepper.

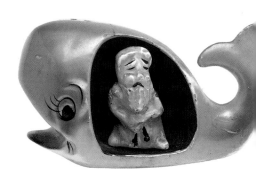

Celebrity Shakes

The unpredictable vitality of American entrepreneurship came alive in the 1940s and 1950s with the production of shakers designed to promote American products from peanuts and flour mixes to cigarettes and dogfood. Light in weight, hospitable to primary colors, and inexpensive to manufacture, plastic was widely used in shakers designed for advertising. The Fiedler and Fiedler Mold and Die Works of Dayton, Ohio, manufactured a variety of plastic sets used by such companies as Campbell Soup, General Mills, and R. J. Reynolds for premiums or giveaways. Because paint was applied *over* solid-colored plastic, paint wear on F&F Co. sets is very common. Items such as Aunt Jemima and Uncle Mose shakers produced in the 1950s and bearing the "F&F Co." logo on the bottom of each set were ultimately found to be racially objectionable and discontinued.

Less controversial shakers manufactured by the F&F Co. were the bright-eyed, cherubic Campbell Soup Kids, Willie and Millie Penguin salt and peppers produced in the early 1940s to promote the iceberg-fresh taste of Kool cigarettes, and Fido and Fifi, an endearing black and yellow pair produced in the 1950s for the Ken-L Ration Pet Food Company. Although most shakers promoting a corporate image or logo were authorized, an occasional bootleg issue has been detected. A set of unauthorized plastic H. J. Heinz ketchup bottles made in Hong Kong surfaced on the retail market in the late 1970s.

Among the most novel advertising shakers are the combination washer-dryer set bearing the Westinghouse imprint (available in forest green and fire engine red script), a pair copyrighted in 1965 by Kentucky Fried Chicken depicting Colonel Harland Sanders, and Pillsbury's flour children, Poppin' and Poppie Fresh. Perhaps the nuttiest and most varied advertising shaker is Mr. Peanut, who made his debut as a trademark for the Planter's Peanut Company of Wilkes-Barre, Pennsylvania, in 1916. Manufactured since the 1930s in a number of styles and delicious colors from peach to pea green, Mr. Peanut shakers are available in both the "crossed" and "uncrossed" leg variety. They were distributed as wrapper premiums and are still relatively easy to find.

A cast of fictional heroes from Mother Goose stories and Walt Disney cartoons have been immortalized in shaker miniatures. Nursery rhyme and storybook characters—Old King Cole, Jonah and the Whale, Mary and Her Lamb, Humpty Dumpty, and others—predominated in the 1930s and 1940s. Hull produced a large line of fairy-tale salt and peppers and, in 1943, made Red Riding Hood shakers, which featured a delicately painted lightweight ceramic.

The television age of the 1950s generated the production of shakers representing cartoon characters including Popeye and Olive Oyl, Donald Duck, Mickey and Minnie Mouse, and Howdy Doody. Although many of these sets are marked as authentic, beginning in the 1940s, Japanese companies flooded the market with unauthorized knock-offs for most of the Disney family. Beswick China, an English manufacturer acquired by Doulton in the 1960s, made bone china sets of Laurel and Hardy and Howdy Doody; colorful and displaying zany facial features, these sets are rarely seen and fetch premium prices.

In 1937, the Borden Company promoted milk products by commissioning a two-piece (head and neck) ceramic shaker of Elsie, the Borden Cow. This was only the beginning of the company's growing line of ceramic shakers. By the late 1940s, even Borden could not resist the allure of marriage and procreation that swept across postwar America. Touting the virtues of the nuclear family as much as their line of dairy products, in the mid-1940s Borden added shakers of Elsie's husband, Elmer, and baby, Beauregard. Ceramic was also used for chocolate-colored shakers shaped like Hershey kisses (sans silver foil and paper wick), sold as souvenirs exclusively at the company's chocolate factory in Hershey, Pennsylvania. Not surprisingly, novelty companies also used glass to manufacture shakers shaped like Pepsi and 7-Up bottles.

When it comes to the world of alcoholic beverages, miniature beer shakers are without peer in their variety. Between 1933 and 1963, two novelty companies, Edward A. Muth & Sons, Inc., of Buffalo, New York, and Bill's Novelty and Premium Company of Milwaukee, Wisconsin, flooded the shaker market with mini-beers representing breweries from more than thirty states, the District of Columbia, and several foreign countries. Purchased by breweries and used as premiums or giveaways, the Muth mini-beers all had metal salt and pepper caps. Many of the shakers made by Bill's Novelty, on the other hand, contained a liquid to represent beer and were distributed with solid caps. Breweriana aficionados are particularly fond of collecting rare, more esoteric mini-beers, among them E&O, Gold Bond, Ruppert, Blatz Pilsener, and the 4¼″ Falstaff. Mini-beers with metal caps and the manufacturer's name embossed on the bottom are more valuable and difficult to find than the "knock-off" shakers with plastic caps made in Taiwan during the 1970s.

Manufactured by F&F Mold and Die Works, the plastic Ken-L-Ration dog and cat were available as premiums in the 1950s. Ceramic sets of Smokey the Bear were available at tourist outposts throughout the West until the mid-1960s.

Celebrities in shaker land range from a rare cast-iron set of President John F. Kennedy, to plastic sets of the Campbell's Soup Kids and the Pillsbury Dough Children. Nursery favorites Humpty Dumpty, Alice, and the Mad Hatter are joined by comic stars Snuffy Smith and Barney Google.

Plastic sets of Mr. Peanut were manufactured beginning in the late 1930s. They are available in several colors including red, yellow, peach, black, and silver. Elsie the Borden Cow originated in 1937 and was eventually joined in future sets by husband, Elmer, and baby, Beauregard. Another heroine of the 1930s, Little Orphan Annie, is accompanied by her faithful mutt, Sandy.

13

Wacky Ware

Exotic or erotic, wacky shakers bypass the superego altogether and travel directly to the id, where they tickle the imagination

The skunk and "cent" coin represent an entire line of shakers in which salt and pepper are connected through a visual or verbal pun.

Wacky Ware

More curious than celebrity shakers of Elsie or the Ken-L Ration dogs, however, are sets that bypass the superego altogether and travel directly to the id, where they tickle the human humor center. Ranging from the erotic to the exotic, wacky salt and peppers include naked figures framed in keyholes or sunning on the beach as well as an entire line of shakers in which salt and pepper—a skunk and a "cent" coin, for example—are connected to each other through a visual or verbal pun. Some shakers in this category draw on hedonistic excesses (martini glass and aspirin tablet) for narrative impact, while others illustrate popular aphorisms. Vallona Starr, a California manufacturer, produced a number of humor-oriented shakers during the 1950s, including a two-piece set available in various colors featuring a Martian piloting a flying saucer. In another Starr set, a woman clutching a rolling pin stands guard over her husband who peers sheepishly from inside a doghouse.

Figural and novelty shakers can be seen as a cultural microcosm, a miniaturized projection of the way we view the world. With their scorching pigments and quirky narrative twists, salt and peppers occupy a unique niche in the decorative arts. In no other utilitarian object in the history of design have art, culture, architecture, and gastronomy been brought into such intimate contact. In short, shakers reflect our whims, passions, and achievements. And besides, when the Martians come to visit, they'll have something to take back home with them.

President Jimmy Carter may have been the role model for a zany pair of salt and pepper shakers. Bodies "California Style" are celebrated by ceramic shakers, while domestic strife gets its due in other pairs.

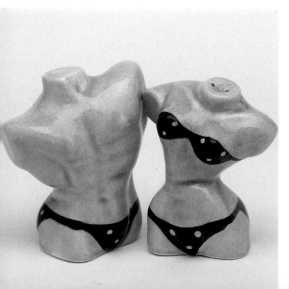

Nude in the keyhole is an inspired entry to the erotic-exotic theme, while planetary shakers pay direct homage to the salt of the earth.

Acknowledgments

The author is deeply indebted to the large number of salt and pepper collectors who, with great patience and enthusiasm, not only lent treasured objects for photographic documentation but who unselfishly gave of their time and shared invaluable personal recollections of the salt and pepper trade. In this regard, I am particularly grateful to Delrae Dorrell, Mattie Dolby, Dawn Wilson, Velma Robinson, Ethel King, Georgia Ludwig, Barbara Spears, John Gramstad, Walter Pelett, Pam Smith, Kari Stanley, Miriam Seger, Roger Margolis, Katherine Dunn, Barbara Goldstein, John Pastier, and Robert Hamilton.

For providing logistic support, I am also indebted to a number of commercial enterprises including the Village Hen, Radical Chic, Habromania, and City Liquidators of Portland, Oregon. Very special thanks are in order for Carey Wong of Theta Production Associates, who designed and constructed a number of elements for the scale models used in the shaker dioramas. The religious diorama was conceived originally by Mr. Wong for The Arkansas Opera Theater production of *Tosca*; the multicolored sculptural panels used in the nightclub diorama were first used in a scale model for the Eugene Opera production of *The Magic Flute*. The rural backdrop for the pigpen diorama was designed by Sandra Kaufman of Theta Productions for the Portland Opera As-

sociation's production of Tchaikovsky's *Eugene Onegin*. Thanks to Carrie Fredinburg of Beaverton Bakery for her help with the wedding cake diorama.

A book of this kind inevitably draws on a very special group of committed friends, advisors, and professionals. Deepest thanks are due especially to Professor Lena Lencek of Reed College, who graciously lent her talents for the conception, design, painting, and final execution of several of the salt and pepper dioramas. Special thanks in this regard also go to Jeremy Kassen and Dorka Bosker.

A number of published sources were also very helpful: Melva Davern, *Salt and Pepper Shakers* (Paducah, Kentucky: Collector Books, 1985); Andrea DiNoto, *Art Plastic: Designed for Living* (New York: Abbeville Press, 1984); Marian Klamkin, *Made in Occupied Japan* (New York: Crown Publishers, 1976); and Dolores H. Simon, *Shawnee Pottery* (Paducah, Kentucky: Collector Books, 1980).

Finally, I am especially grateful to my editor Sarah Kirshner and the book's designer Howard Morris who, as collaborators in the fullest sense, helped this project take on a delicious life of its own.